Moving On

by

Alan Gibbons

Illustrated by Julia Page

First published in 2009 in Great Britain by
Barrington Stoke Ltd
18 Walker Street, Edinburgh, EH3 7LP

www.barringtonstoke.co.uk

ISBN: 978-1-84299-617-1

Printed in Great Britain by Bell & Bain Ltd

A Note from the Author

This book tells the story of two Travellers. Minty is an English Romany Gypsy and her friend Danny is an Irish Traveller. Both are made up. The events in my story are made up too. I learned about young English and Irish Travellers by talking to them. I've done my best to be true to what they told me. Any mistakes are mine.

Alan Gibbons

With special thanks to the London Gypsy and Traveller Unit

Contents

Chapter 1
Minty

I got into trouble at school again. It was last Monday. It had been building up all day. The problem was the supply teacher, Mrs Green. She was so boring I felt like crying. She didn't try to make the lesson interesting at all. I never thought I'd miss Mrs Jackson so much. She's good fun ... for a teacher. But Mrs Green wasn't. She just read stuff from a book. She went on and on. Boring. That's not teaching. I could do that myself!

Well, I got the fidgets, the way you do. I just couldn't sit still any more. Soon I was passing silly notes to my friends. It wasn't long before we were giggling and poking each other. You know how it goes.

Mrs Green was staring at me. She didn't look at the other kids – just me. She's taken our class once or twice before and I don't think she's ever liked me. I think she's got a problem because I'm a Traveller. It happens.

So she comes over, doesn't she? I wasn't the only one messing about but she came straight up to me. She just wants to sit at her desk and talk at us. As if we're a row of potatoes. But I can't sit still, so I'm messing up her day.

She looks down her nose at me and says, "Be quiet!"

I started to argue back. That's something potatoes never do. I wasn't being rude, I just wanted to talk about what we were doing. That didn't go down well, of course. Next thing you know, she's shouting at me at the top of her voice.

"You'll do what I say, young lady," she says.

I couldn't help myself. I was so fed up, I laughed in her face.

Well, she went mad. I didn't mean to upset her. But she was so over the top. She was wagging her finger at me and her voice went all high and squeaky. Mrs Jackson never acts like that. If we play up, she takes us to one side and talks to us softly, one to one. She treats us like people, not potatoes.

Mrs Green was different. She just kept on getting louder and louder. What did she think I'd do? I wasn't going to sit there and take it, was I? Mrs Green doesn't know me very well. It turned into a real shouting match. I gave out as good as I got.

Then she turned away from me. I thought it was over but I was wrong. She was just by her desk when she said it –

"You people."

She thought I hadn't heard her but I was straight out of my chair. I asked what she meant and her face went white. She knew she'd gone too far and she might be in trouble herself.

"What do you mean, *you people?*" I wanted to know.

She didn't say much after that but I knew why she said it. Because I'm a Traveller. I've had to put up with this stuff before. To make things worse, the Head of Year put me on report after that.

It isn't right. I've been trying really hard in school. I was in a bad mood all the way home. What have people got against us? We're the same as anyone else. We want somewhere to live. We want to earn a living. We want respect.

That doesn't sound like much to ask, does it? But no one knows anything about the travelling people. They don't know what we want or what we need. There are so many people like Mrs Green, who don't know who we are, where we came from or how we live. They don't make any effort to find out.

For starters, people use the word Gypsy as an insult. Mrs Green didn't come right out with it and call me 'dirty Gypsy' or anything like that, but I bet that's what she was thinking.

I come from a Romany family with a long history and that makes me a Gypsy. But it's the way people say the word that bothers me. They spit it out as if it's something rude – something to be ashamed of. Then there are the other insults. I don't like being called a 'Gyppo' or a 'Pikey'. That's out of order. When people start calling us names, they're saying we're different. They're saying we're not as good as they are. That there's something wrong with us.

People like Mrs Green don't come out with it like the loud-mouths but they've still got this picture in their head. They think we're violent or that we're robbers, trouble-makers. But all we want is a peaceful life. And our lives seem to be getting harder.

I'm Minty, by the way. I'm 15. I've got two sisters, Alice and Kate, and two brothers, Freddie and Henry. Henry's the oldest and he's named after my dad, like a lot of the boys are. I've lived all my life on a caravan site in south London. My family always moved around in the old days, but we have to stay put a lot longer these days. There are all sorts of laws being used to change our way of life.

You hear people say you can't be a real Gypsy if you live on a permanent site. People think to be a real Gypsy you have to be on the move all the time. It's not true. I've never lived by the road-side but my old nan was born in a horse-drawn wagon. That's my nan in the corner. She still does crafts. She's really good with her hands. She makes holly rings – like you have on doors at Christmas. She also makes wooden flowers just like they did in the old days. She makes them by curling the wood. Then she dyes them different colours.

When she gets talking about the old days, it makes me feel sad. It sounds so free, the way she lived when she was young. She talks about the old way of life. Her family moved on from place to place, stopping on the old Commons. Her eyes light up when she starts talking about the Horse Fairs and the big weddings they had. She says it's a lost world.

It's a different kind of life for us young ones. We have to live on permanent sites because we're not allowed to move around any more. There aren't many places to stop along the road. There aren't many places on Council caravan sites either, so some Travellers have to live in houses. That doesn't mean they've stopped being Travellers. It doesn't make any difference to the way they see themselves. As soon as you meet them you just know they're Travellers. It's the whole way they behave.

I'll give you an example. I bet Mrs Green would be surprised to know that Romany people have got strong moral values. Boys and girls don't sleep in the same caravan. Traveller families often have loads of children. Our families love their children and we like nothing better than sitting together, laughing and joking and telling stories. We're really close. Most times the men work and the women stay at home. Once they're 13, the girls are in charge of cleaning and looking after the younger children. The boys will work too – as soon as they get to be 13. I'm proud of the way we live.

I spend a lot of time with my mum and my nan. We sit on the step and talk for hours. I listen to them talk about their lives and the way they grew up and I see myself in them. I watch them getting on with their jobs around the site and I know that's the way I'll be a few years from now. That's the way things are. It's our way of life.

Then ... then sometimes I feel different. At school, the girls I hang out with start talking about college and careers and I get this odd tingly feeling. Am I excited for them, or scared, or jealous even? I don't know. Maybe I just think too much.

I like going to the Bingo with my mum and my nan. People are very welcoming at the Bingo. They don't treat you any different. They don't start saying you're causing trouble or leaving a mess. They just accept you for what you are. That's all we want, a bit of respect for the way we live.

But, with people like Mrs Green, you know you've got to fight for it.

What is a Gypsy?

Romany Gypsies came from northern India to start with. Over a thousand years ago they started moving around and living in tents. They never stayed anywhere for long. They are the biggest group of Travellers in the UK.

Romany Gypsies don't have anything to do with Rome or Romania.

The word Gypsy comes from a mistake. Some people thought Romany Gypsies came from Egypt and called them Egyptians. Over time, this got shortened to Gypsy.

Romany Gypsies speak a language called Romani. It comes from a very old Indian language – Sanskrit.

Gypsies are not 'foreign'. They don't come from another country. They have been in Britain since 1515. The first Gypsies in England arrived when Henry VIII was king – 500 years ago.

In Ireland the first Gypsies arrived even longer ago – back in the 1100s.

Gypsies are not 'dirty'. They're very strict about being clean, with all sorts of rules and different words like mokadi and mahrime to tell you how things should be done. There are strict rules about what things you can wash in what bowls.

In 1547 King Edward VI passed a law which said that Gypsies had to be made into slaves for two years. If they escaped they would be made slaves for life.

In 1554 Queen Mary I made a law to say Gypsies could be put to death for entering the country.

The last Gypsy to be put to death in England was in the 1650s when Oliver Cromwell ran the country.

What about the Roma?

The Roma are Romany Gypsies who have come to the UK from Eastern Europe in the last few years.

Everyone knows that Hitler killed millions of Jews during the Second World War. But did you know that the Nazis also killed between **220,000** and **500,000** Roma and Sinti Gypsies?

And even after the War many Roma escaped to the UK as refugees because they were being badly treated in the countries where they were living.

Chapter 2
Danny

"Are you all right?"

The lad asking me was Danny Donelly, a mate of mine. I met up with him after school.

"I'm OK," I said.

"You don't look it," Danny said. "You look rubbish."

So I told him what happened with Mrs Green.

Danny's an Irish Traveller. I met him at Epsom a few months back. Epsom's one of the last big Horse Fairs. All us Travellers park on a field when we go there. We have to pay between 50 and 200 quid for that.

The English and Irish Travellers didn't mix that much when Mum and Nan were young. It's different for us. A load of us met up in a big group at Epsom. The thing is – it's good to be together and we like the Traveller lifestyle. It's good to hang out with people who know what makes you tick.

Danny and me hit it off right away and we've been friends since the fair. In the old days Irish Travellers were tinkers and they sold things door-to-door. Now his family earns a living working on the roads and driveways. Sometimes they do brickwork fencing. He lives on a site in London – like we do. Danny's a few months older than me. He comes from a big family too. There are seven of them.

"Forget about it," Danny said when I told him about Mrs Green. "There's a lot worse than her." He gave a shrug. "Don't worry about it – maybe you won't see her again."

"She comes in quite a lot," I told him. "I don't think she's going to go away."

"So?" Danny said. "Just ignore her."

I wish it was that easy. She's the one who picked a fight with me. But Danny was right about there being worse people than Mrs Green, though. His family's been having trouble where they live. Their site's in the middle of nowhere. They're stuck under a fly-over and there's nothing nearby, no shops or schools – nothing like that. As we near his site, the local pubs have been putting up signs saying things like 'No Gypsies'. It's illegal to do that but it still happens.

That's not all. Danny's family has had other troubles since they came here. People came down a while ago with baseball bats. Someone sneaked up to one of the trailers and tried to light the gas bottle Danny's family uses for cooking. What if it had exploded? There were people inside the trailer at the time. Someone could have been badly hurt.

"What makes them so angry and full of hate?" Danny asked me. "Did I tell you about what happened to one of our lads the other week?" he went on.

I shook my head.

"A group of men outside one of the pubs shouted over at one of our lads," Danny told me. "They were all friendly and grinning at this lad. But when he walked over to them, they took out a knife and slashed his face."

It's terrible but it doesn't surprise me.
I've seen the same sort of stuff myself. There
are the people like Mrs Green who have a
bad attitude but never say anything out loud.
Then there are the people who are happy to
pick a fight with us, or worse.

"The Shades were no good," Danny said.
"They acted like we caused the trouble. Like
it was our fault."

The Shades is what Danny calls the police. That or the Warbs. I worry about him sometimes. One of these days he'll say it too loud and get himself into trouble. He's got a temper, a bit like me really. My mum and dad say the police are a lot better than they used to be, but they still drive up and down and stare at you like you're doing something wrong.

We went over to Danny's site after that. When we got there, everyone made me feel welcome. I almost forgot about Mrs Green. Family is important for Irish Travellers, just like it is for us. I love getting up in the morning with all my family drinking tea and having a chat. It's great having your family around you, knowing you can go anywhere you want. You step outside the door and there they are – everyone who belongs to you. If you visit another Traveller, they'll tell you to sleep anywhere. They'll say, "Make yourself welcome."

Danny told his dad what happened to me at school.

"Been a bit too gobby, have you, Minty?" he said, winking.

He's got me right. But sometimes you have to stick up for yourself.

The women on Danny's site mostly stay at home, same as the ones on ours. Sometimes they tell fortunes or sell lucky charms, like in the old days. I'm not sure that's what I want to do with my life. But what else do I do?

I sat watching the kids play. Maybe that's what I'll spend my life doing – like my mum – watching the kids.

Some of the kids were using a few words of *Gammon*. Romany Gypsies aren't the only ones with their own language. Irish Travellers speak their own secret language.

"Your Mrs Green should come down here
and see what we're really like," Danny said.
"She might learn something. I hate the way
people talk about us and don't even bother to
find out what we're really like."

I couldn't help giggling. He stopped and
looked over at me.

"What are you laughing at?" he asked.

"Just look at you!" I said. "I've started you off now. You should go into politics and be an M.P. or something."

"That's not a bad idea," Danny grunted. "Someone needs to stick up for Travellers. We always get a bad name. Even when it's something stupid like a kid's ball going missing, people will pick out a Traveller to blame."

Suddenly I'm thinking about Mrs Green again.

Who are the Irish Travellers?

The first people talked about the Irish Travellers was a thousand years ago. They spoke a language called Shelta. Later on this got mixed with some Romani and became a language called Gammon.

Some people say the Irish Travellers were once poets who moved from place to place with their poems and songs. Others say they were Irish Lords who had lost their lands.

Chapter 3
The Trouble with School

Our normal teacher was back the next day. That's Mrs Jackson. On the way out to break she came over to talk to me.

"Why don't you tell me what happened yesterday?" she asked. "Mrs Green was very upset."

I tried to explain but she didn't look happy.

"Are you sure you heard Mrs Green right?" she asked.

"I heard what she said," I told her, "and the way she said it. I know what she meant."

"What about you?" Mrs Jackson asked. "Do you think you did the right thing?"

I gave a shrug.

"Let's say for a minute that you were right about what she said," Mrs Jackson went on. "Don't you think there might be a better way of dealing with it?"

I gave another shrug.

"You're a bright girl, Minty," Mrs Jackson said with a sigh in her voice. "You could do well if you wanted. Don't throw it away."

She left it at that. A lot of Travellers have a bad time in school. It's hard when your parents and grandparents don't know much about school. My nan still doesn't read and write. They sent her to school when she was little but it didn't work.

"It was as if there was something blocking the way to school – like an invisible rope across the school door," she said. "I don't think I ever really got past that rope." She found it that hard ever to go into school.

Things are better now but not that much. I've always been a bit on edge at school. It's hard to fit in when your way of life is totally different from everyone else.

Quite often, Travellers just don't see what school's got to offer us. We learn about life from our own people – how to bring up a family, how to make a living for yourself, the kind of values you should have. Mum and Dad are very worried about how they teach you about sex and drugs in school. They don't think it's right to tell children all that stuff.

But school's difficult for us because of other things too. In primary school, they kept trying to make me do things their way. It felt as if they were always nagging me. I was only little and used to running free. I'd never had to sit still or stay in one place for so long. School was different to the way things were at home, and there was no give and take. It was their way or nothing at all.

One day I got up in the middle of class and said I was off home. One of the teachers had to chase after me! She got in front of me and crouched down like a goalkeeper. I saw the light between her legs and made my bid for freedom. I tried to duck under her skirt. I got caught up in it and she fell on her backside with her legs in the air. She turned as red as a beetroot.

It wasn't all my fault. My teachers never asked me what was wrong. They never seemed to think they had to meet me half-way.

Apart from that primary school was all right. Some of the teachers made a real effort and I liked having one class teacher who looked after me every day.

Secondary school has been much more difficult. I like subjects like Drama, IT, Art and Science when you get to do something instead of just sitting there. But I don't like it when you just have to listen to someone talking. It's so boring. Teachers get angry with you if you get up and move around. That's how the trouble with Mrs Green started.

Then there's the bullying. It isn't all the kids. Some are nice. But it only takes a few to spoil things. There was a girl called Suzanne at my last school. She must have heard words like 'Pikey' and 'Gyppo' at home. When I was in Year Eight she started saying them softly – so I could just make them out. Just because I wasn't reading as quickly as her, she started to call me stupid. I went for her over that. Guess what? I was the one who got sent to the Head Teacher! The teachers thought I was causing trouble all the time. I just lost interest.

I moved schools last year. My new school is much better. I get on OK with a few of the girls and that stops any name-calling. The teachers seem to care a bit more too. And I like Mrs Jackson. I don't know if that will make much difference when it comes to exams and stuff like that.

Sometimes I think I'd like to get a job. Maybe I could work with other Travellers trying to help the younger kids find a way to fit in. But I don't know of many Traveller women who've gone to college or had a career. It's a big step. I don't know if I can do it.

Danny's always saying I can do anything if I put my mind to it. None of his family can read or write but he's a great reader. You should hear the books he's read. The older people never had the time for school. But he's bright and keen to learn.

He says he always liked school until
something went missing a few weeks ago and
one of the other boys said he'd taken it.
Danny said that no one was going to call him
a thief. He told them he wasn't going back to
school any more. He's been off school ever
since, working with his dad and brothers. I
don't know if he'll ever go back. A lot of
Travellers never do. Danny's funny. He tells
me I should stick at it then he walks out
himself! What do you make of that?

Are there any famous Gypsies?

There are plenty of people who are Romany or Irish Travellers and who've done really well. There have been artists, writers, scientists, musicians and singers, even MPs in Hungary and Spain. Here are some famous people from Traveller backgrounds that you might have heard of.

Sir Charles Chaplin. He was known as Charlie Chaplin when he was a famous film star. He starred in some old films like The Great Dictator and Modern Times. He became Sir Charles Chaplin in 1975.

Sir Michael Caine. Another movie actor, Sir Michael Caine. He's won two Oscars and was made a knight in 2000.

Bob Hoskins. When he was young, Bob travelled a lot and worked in a circus. He became an actor and has starred in movies like The Long Good Friday.

Elvis Presley. The King of Rock and Roll came from the Sinti people. He had many hit records and starred in films.

Eric Cantona. Cantona played football for France. He also helped Manchester United win their first Premiership title in 26 years.

Freddie Eastwood. Freddie is a Romany Gypsy. He's famous for scoring the only goal when Southend United beat Manchester United.

Jose Antonio Reyes used to play for Arsenal. He now plays for Real Madrid and Spain.

Shayne Ward. Shayne won The X Factor on TV. He is now a big pop star.

Chapter 4
A Lucky Escape

Danny had a lucky escape last week. He'd come to see us on the way back from work. He was with his dad and brothers. We were still busy around the site and Danny wanted something to do so he went to the shop for a bar of chocolate.

There was a gang of lads hanging round the door of the shop. One of them was the boy who'd accused him of stealing at school.

Danny didn't take any notice of them at first. He just pushed past and went inside. The shop-keeper was watching him like a hawk.

"Are you from up the road?" he asked.

Danny didn't like the way he said it.

"What's that supposed to mean?" he asked.

"You know what I'm talking about," the shop-keeper said. "I hope you're going to pay for that bar of chocolate."

That set Danny off. It was just like that day in school he told me about. He slapped the chocolate bar on the counter and waved a ten pound note.

"Is that good enough for you?" he snapped.

The shop-keeper took the money and gave Danny his change. As Danny was walking out, the shop-keeper said something very softly. It was just like my run-in with Mrs Green. Danny spun round.

"What did you say?" he asked.

He should have just carried on walking. He knows that now. But you know Danny.

The moment the words were out of his mouth, the gang of lads moved in. They'd been waiting for Danny to do something.

"Is he giving you trouble?" they asked the shop-keeper. "He was stealing stuff at school too."

The shop-keeper didn't answer them. But they weren't going to let it go.

"We don't like your sort round here," they said.

That again. You people. Your sort. Danny was looking for a way out.

"I don't want any trouble," he told them.

"Tough," the ring-leader said. "You've got it."

The ring-leader put his hand into his jacket. Maybe it was a bluff – but Danny wasn't taking any chances. He knew he had to do something quickly. He shoved the ring-leader and made a run for it. They went after him. Luckily, Danny's a good runner.

As soon as we saw him sprinting down the road towards us, we knew something was wrong. Danny's dad and brothers jumped up. So did my two brothers, Freddie and Henry. The whole lot of them are boxers and they look like it. The gang got the message. They skidded to a halt. They shouted a few things then they turned round and walked back towards the shops.

When we asked Danny what happened, he just shook his head. He only told us later. I knew he was thinking about what happened to Johnny Delaney.

Who was Johnny Delaney?

Johnny Delaney was kicked to death on the outskirts of Ellesmere Port near Liverpool in May 2003. It happened after an argument with a group of teenagers.

He was only 15 and he came from an Irish Traveller family.

The killers got four years.

They said Johnny was "only a Gypsy."

The judge said there wasn't enough evidence to prove that it was a racist attack.

Johnny's father Patrick said, "There's no justice here. They were kicking my son like a football. Are they going to let this happen to another Gypsy?"

Chapter 5
New Memories to Make

I really like Danny's older sister Kathleen. She came round to Danny's last week with her husband Paddy and her three kids. They're all lovely and the baby, Kevin, is so sweet. He's got huge, pale blue eyes.

Kathleen was really down in the dumps. When her and Paddy got married they had to move off the site. The council put them in a B&B hotel. Their room was really small and damp and there was nowhere to put anything. They've got a flat now. It's much nicer, but it's a long way from the caravan site where the rest of the family live.

"I'm always coming round to my mum's," Kathleen said. "It's lonely over in my flat. A woman called me names in the street the other day. I'd rather be here, close to my own people."

"I don't know why you put up with it," Danny said. "No one should be forced to live in a house or a flat if they don't want to. You should have the choice to live in a trailer. What's everyone got to be grounded for?"

Danny's mum agreed. "I worry for the young people," she said. "They're trying to do away with the travelling people. But we know ourselves and we know how we want to live. When we were moving around, every day was different. Life made sense then."

She shook her head sadly. "Just look at Kathleen and Paddy. They're not happy living in a flat. When you're stuck in one place, you feel grounded. We need to travel. If we don't, there's no new memories being made."

That had a big effect on me, what she said. She's right. We're being forced to give up our way of life. What if, in a few years' time, the young ones have forgotten the Traveller way of life? What if there's no work for them, and no people of their own any more?

"Do you remember when I said you should be an M.P., Danny?" I said. "I'm serious. Someone's got to do something."

"Not me," Danny said. "I'll be too busy working with my dad and my brothers."

"So you're not going back to school?" I asked.

He shook his head. "What's the point? I'm just going to get along, making a living."

I tried to argue with him.

"Forget it," he said. "You're looking at the wrong person. I've tried doing things the way the country people want." That's what Danny calls non-Travellers – 'country people'. "It didn't work, did it?" he went on. "I'm never going to be part of their world. We've got our way of life. They've got theirs. End of story."

I shook my head. "I don't think it's that easy, Danny," I said. "You know what's going on. The world's destroying the travelling life. You can't just look the other way. If we don't stick up for ourselves, everything we care about will be dead and gone. We've got to do something."

Kathleen looked at me. "Are you serious?" she asked. "You really want to do something about the way we've got to live?"

I nodded.

"Then you should go and see Patsy Rooney," Kathleen said.

"Who's she?" I asked.

"Oh, Patsy works with Travellers," Kathleen said. "She's an Irish Traveller herself. She's the one who got us out of that B&B. She runs a youth club for the kids. You'd like her."

So I went down to meet Patsy on Monday. I skipped school to do it. It wasn't a difficult choice. I thought Mrs Green might be in again.

I had to wait to talk to Patsy because she was really busy. People were calling in to talk to her and ringing her on the phone. She's making a film with some of the families and she was fixing that up. Just before she got to talk to me, she had to book a mini-bus to take the boys' five-a-side team to a tournament.

When I got to talk to her at last, I told her how I'd been feeling.

"I don't think Travellers should forget who they are," I told her. "We need to remember where we come from."

Patsy smiled. "That sounds good to me." There was a sparkle in her eye. "So what are you going to do about it?"

"I don't know," I said. "I was hoping you'd tell me."

"If a thing is worth doing," Patsy said, "then it's got to come from inside a person."

I thought about what I was saying. I put what I was feeling into words. "I want to work with the little ones," I said. "I want them to go to school and learn to stand up for themselves."

"And are you going to school?" Patsy asked. "It's a school day today."

I must have gone red because she started to laugh.

"You can't go telling other people what to do if you don't do it yourself," she said.

I knew she was right. I thought the same thing when Danny was telling me what to do.

That was the moment everything fell into place. So what if not many Travellers know how to read and write? It's got to start somewhere. Why not with me?

"I'm doing all right at school," I told Patsy. "I don't give it a miss very often. Now I'm going to do better."

She nodded. "I'm sure you are," she said.

Are things getting any better?

The Caravan Sites Act ordered councils, from 1970, to provide caravan sites for Travellers in England. It was a step forward.

In 1994 this changed. The Criminal Justice Act abolished the Caravan Sites Act. It left at least **5,000** families with no legal home.

Families can be made to move on if no one wants them around.

The council can take away their things.

Young married couples are being forced to live in flats or B&B hotels because there's no room on the caravan sites. It's causing a lot of unhappiness.

Chapter 6
Time to Fight

You won't believe who was back in school today. It was Mrs Green. I couldn't believe it. I didn't want to see her again. She wasn't covering for Mrs Jackson this time. She was teaching History instead. Guess what? She did the same thing as last time – sat at the desk and read out of a book. That's all she ever does. And she gets paid for it!

It wasn't long before some of the kids started messing about. Mrs Green looked right at me. She was waiting for me to join in so she could report me. Well, not this time, I thought. I'm not falling for it.

The noise in the classroom got louder and louder. Mrs Green started shouting again. It's an odd idea, isn't it? She thinks she can make kids shut up by getting louder herself? Weird!

Anyway, after a bit the Head of Year walked in the room. He wanted to know what was going on. He remembered he'd put me on report on Monday and he looked across at me. Mrs Green had to tell him I was one of the ones who was behaving herself. That must have hurt. She looked like a dog chewing a wasp.

I bumped into Mrs Jackson on my way to English.

"I heard what happened in Mrs Green's lesson," she said. "I'm really proud of you."

She was walking away when she remembered something.

"Don't forget your course work is due in," she said.

I reached down into my bag to get it and I handed it to her.

"I finished it last night," I told her.

You should have seen the smile on her face. I think we both knew I'd won.

Danny came round this evening. He isn't going back to school. He's going to work with his dad and brothers. He's made his choice. I've made mine. I told him how I want to pass my exams and go to college.

"Then I can work with the children," I said. "I can make a difference."

Danny had this big grin on his face.

"Good on you," he said. "What made your mind up?"

"It was something your mum said," I told him. "I just got this feeling. It's time to fight for our way of life. It's time to make some new memories."

Some Romani words we use in everyday language

Pal

Lollipop

Kushti – what Del Boy in Only Fools and Horses says to mean 'good'.

Hickory, Dickory, Dock is Romany for 'one o'clock, two o'clock'.

AUTHOR FACT FILE
ALAN GIBBONS

Did you have a favourite teacher, and if so why?

My favourite teacher was an English teacher called Tom Potts. He was a bit different and a bit weird but he must have done something right. Now my job is writing books!

What inspired you to write this book?

I really hate it when people don't get a fair deal so I thought it was a good idea to think up a story about Travellers.

What new things did you learn about Travellers when writing this book?

I didn't know how many Travellers can't move around any more.

What is your favourite part of Traveller life?

My favourite parts are the moving around even if that's not happening much any more. The other thing I think is great is that your family is so important.

ILLUSTRATOR FACT FILE
JULIA PAGE

Did you ever get in trouble at school?

Yes, often! I think it was because I was taller than the other girls ... and so the teachers always saw me.

Did you have a favourite teacher, and if so why?

My art teacher! She always helped me with my work and was kind and friendly. I think she liked me and knew art was important to me.

What new things did you learn about Travellers when illustrating this book?

Travellers are proud of their history and their way of life. They want the rest of us to understand about their customs and lives. Often they get treated unfairly because people don't know anything about them.

What is your favourite part of Traveller life?

I like the way they stick together and how they think that families are so important.

Barrington Stoke would like to thank all its readers for commenting on the manuscript before publication and in particular:

Samad Abdul

Danielle Argent

Jack Carlisle

Nathaniel Clegg

Jemma Defries

Marian Mahoney

Michelle Mahoney

Zumer Malek

Jacqueline Maughan

Laura Maughan

Martin Maughan

Terence Maughan

Holly McGuinness

Daniel Mongan

Richard Mongan

Andrew Nicolls

Ben Parkinson

David Regis-Hanrahan

Laura Smith

Lisa Smith

Louise Smith

Viner Smith

Amy Taggart

Melisa Umwiza

Jaymes Venables

Become a Consultant!

Would you like to give us feedback on our titles before they are published? Contact us at the email address below – we'd love to hear from you!

info@barringtonstoke.co.uk
www.barringtonstoke.co.uk

Try another book in the "FYI" series!
Fiction with stacks of facts

Codes
Codebreakers
by Deborah Chancellor

Maths
Counting on Leroy
by Steve Mills and Hilary Koll

The Romans
Assassin
by Tony Bradman

Surveillance
The Doomsday Watchers
by Steve Barlow and Steve Skidmore

All available from our website:
www.barringtonstoke.co.uk